Crystalized Spoken Words

SPOKEN WORDS

Jacquelyn Rice Dunbar

authorHOUSE®

AuthorHouse™
1663 Liberty Drive
Bloomington, IN 47403
www.authorhouse.com
Phone: 1-800-839-8640

First published by AuthorHouse 4/19/2010

ISBN: 978-1-4490-8667-1 (e)
ISBN: 978-1-4490-8666-4 (sc)

Library of Congress Control Number: 2010904754

Printed in the United States of America
Bloomington, Indiana

This book is printed on acid-free paper.

Contents

About the Author. 1

Special Thanks 2

A Day at the Beach. 3

A Faded Image to the Other Side 4

A Friend. 5

A Parents Foundation 6

A Recipe of Daily Living. 7

A Teachers Compassionate Teaching 8

Admonishing Spirit 9

An Encounter with a little Girl. 10

Appeased. 11

Aspirations 12

Bare Skin 13

Bazaar Disaster. 14

Burning Passion 15

Busy Body 16

Complicated Pleasures 17

Compromise 18

Crystallized Change Coming 19

Don't Go There. 20

Don't Live in Regrets. 21

Don't Walk Away 22

Don't You Dare. 23

Elegance of One 24

Expressions 25

Father versus Daddy 26

First Day at School 27

Forever Imprisoned 28

Genuine Concern 29

Going on your feelings or on one's Faith 30

Hopeful Cause 31

I Missed You 32

I was Just Checking 33

If You Wandered Why 34

Inner Ambition 35

It Stops Right Here 36

Just Your Existence 37

Kisses from the Unknown 38

Let's Try Again 39

Love Hard and Loving Easy 40

Lusting Souls 41

Mathematically Speaking 42

Mesmerize 43

My Dad's Love 44

No Performance 45

Nothing Else Left to Say 46

Obsession 47

Out of Anger 48

Out of Courtesy 49

Perfect Harmony 50

Please Forgive Me 51

Profound Statement 52

Racial Contradictive 53

Rain Down on Me 54

Reaction to your Actions. 55

Rebellious Child. 56

Reposition Oneself. 57

Resolutions 58

Revengeful Heart 59

Romantic Dinner 60

Silent Voice 61

So many Times 62

Soul Search 63

Speaking From the Heart 64

Stepping Out In the Unknown. 65

Stop Judging Ourselves. 66

Stuck on Stupid 67

The Detour 68

The Dire Passion. 69

Trail and Error 70

Tranquilities 71

Triumphs. 72

Undefined Line. 73

Under The Influence 74

Unraveled Spirit. 75

We Will See. 76

What Came Over Me. 77

What Did You Say 78

What is your Given Purpose 79

What Keeps Me Going 80

What Makes You a Delight. 81

What you do to me. 82

When it was all said and Done. 83

When Will It Be 84

When you Lose A Love One. 85
Words. 86
Wrongly Accused. 87
You Knew Nothing 88
You were my First 89
Your Journey. 90

About the Author

I am excited about the continuous endeavors, that my poetry is
going in. I believe, that there is no reason, to not be successful.
You determine your own destination in which you set out on.

Special Thanks

I would first and foremost, like to thank God, for creating and then presuming to give me life. I truly enjoy the opportunity to expressive the inner deepened thoughts that reside inside. For every piece of poetry written, is expression of passions that go underneath the unspoken words exclusively meant for thee.

For every day, I utilize as the opportunity to broaden the intellectual expressions felt from the inner soul. For the inner thoughts that bring about an emotion, knows no certain way, but indulges with deep passions, conveyed words you have chosen to say.

For the time is now, not later, but immediately to speak clearly, so one may get the actual thought that has begin to unfold.

I thank every supportive friend & family that has stood there cheering me in. Every inspiring word spoken to me along the way, has given me an empowered driven force to create more expressive deepened words.

I ceased this moment of reaching out to others, with a clear cut message spoken to you.

For every gifted hand used to combine the finishing touches of this book, I thank you with sincere love from the bottom of my heart.

A Day at the Beach

As the tides blow in all the valleys of water there in ...As the sand is blown by the gusting wind it clashes against the flawless faces of us there in as it sails in....As I sought out the sight I wished to find...The scene gave me a uplifting satisfaction with a great adore.....Easing one's troubled soul to a self reliant incredible soul....

A Faded Image to the Other Side

While driving home, I felt a little lethargic, inside….I repetitiously
convinced myself, that I was almost there and to wake up now….
With much consideration, of the inner thoughts inside, I stepped out
a moment from the inner body and reflected back on what I looked
like…..Astonishing, for a brief moment, that what I just witnessed on
the other side…..While still sleep, I ran off the road gliding along the
sides…Unknowingly, I was headed for a ram in a bush with no turning
back to the other side….Abruptly, a soft whisper, whispered to me,
not yet my sweet child, wake up right now….That is when I woke up
immediately, displaced for a minute on just what occurred in a moment
ago to me….A faded image of where I thought I was going, was
conveyed to me….Rather later and not now transferred to me…..

A Friend

One who knows and cares of what hurts you have let truth be known….They stick around, when everyone else seemly vanishes away….When no one was there to lend a listening ear, they were there giving you one to hear…When a tear was shed, you were standing near ready to wipe them away….When I had made a mistake, you were there to lift me up….Never telling a story, but telling me what was right and saying I am still here alright …..You were one in a million, because; no one had this quality within…Just a special person that cared deep within…

A Parents Foundation

As a parent, we set a foundation, to guide our children with great
intentions of proper success ...As they began to grow, the changes
transfer to another never seen before...In the mist of their growth
, we teach them what it is to love, respect, and most importantly
be accountable for their own actions commenced...For so long, we
sheltered them from all the cruelties of the world that awaits them at
the sound of a roar...For , we know one day, , they would have to fly
on their own...Putting it off as long as we could, until, it came along....
As we let go of their tender hands , we rest assure with the thought
of knowing that we soared for more and more in everyway , so that
they would fly, in higher successes they would stick with them forever
more....

A Recipe of Daily Living

A pinch of love in its way….A pinch of inner love, leaves no room for stress to dwell…A pinch of laughter brings about longer jeopardy in living….A pinch of patience, allows the heart grow founder….A pinch of faith, gives one a vision of hopeful anticipations on its way…Now mix all of these together and live one day at a time in stride….

A Teachers Compassionate Teaching

As the teacher opens up with their main objective of what was required of us all….Piece by piece was taught in such a unique way, that you could recite every word that had been contradicted to all the students in its own way…..As the teacher may pardon with its students in a more personalized way…Much emphasis was placed with the adorned depict way….Full of hesitations , with the challenges that may be discouraging to one's ability to absorb new knowledge given unto each student in a continuous way….

Admonishing Spirit

It repetitiously reminds you of where you at and guides you to constant improving for the betterment of self….It uplifts you and in the same sense constructively corrects you when you are wrong….It never keeps a tally of what you have done right or what you have done wrong to be held over your head as you come into the newness of peaceful consist in its own….It surrounds itself with peace that manifests itself into its forever love that never changes in its dignified love….No need to go out on a limb in search too far, for it is available to you right here thus far…..Admonishing Spirit, brings about a transforming conversion ready for you from god as you kneel down and pray …..

An Encounter with a little Girl

I encountered a close relationship with a little girl whom, I discovered had been distorted by something overtaking with the strongest immersing force....So I reached out and allowed my inner compassion to convey to her......No one ever stopped to even wander, or even made time to adjust a little one on one time....My heart grew even more and more....

Appeased

It was your mere being, as you sat foot in the room.....Upon, the open of your mouth, it appeased my inner depths of where my heart absorbed all that you was to me....Your hand, placed into mine, like a solid fit with mine...What a soothing smell you gave off as you came closer to me...One of such driven force, deviled in thee....It was you, I longed for with the deepest confession of such appeased formality you send to me...Just right out appeased by what you are in all its formalities

Aspirations

One may soar low….

One may soar high….

One may combine both and uphold….Which is better, only your preset goals could predict the level of aspirations you chose to uphold…..

Bare Skin

As the bareness of the uniqueness of one's created body…...As each line, has its own curve that rounds itself to your molded figure in thee…... Bare Skin, Bare Skin, full of life and beauty as would unfold….Breathe taken to one as its uniqueness of the curves fitted into one…Smooth skin swaying down one's spine ad intertwine with mine…...Bare skin, Bare skin, one's inner composition that resides there in mine……

Bazaar Disaster

As the earth revolved all around, it came full circle back around rather bazaar…As it tilt a slight but shattered into pieces , giving us a shake for our life, while millions of persons , were thrown all around, they feared the life that was taken for granted up until this driven point… Disaster, has struck at this critical point , leaving numerous persons feeling in despair….The point of it all, the earth and all that it holds, is ruled by a father in the heavens as we looked deeper within….Such a bazaar disaster, no words could explain the event in which was meant to occur….

Burning Passion

The sense of urgency of a burning desire to be driven hard force for more n more...It lingers around in one's head with a driven force from inside my inner soul... It creates inner joys indescribable with amazing immersing distinctive passions with a rather reserved depict with screamed vigorous burning for more ...The formality, was breathe taken as it was sought out with incredible ambitions for even more...

Busy Body

One of volunteered aggression with others daily issues in a rather
disturbing magnified aptitude…No real true compassion of what
others underwent, just selfishly spoken abrupt words in a deranged
formality….Plundering in others endeavors, leaving only less time for
there own realities…Living and hoping through others ambitions of
endeavors earned with dignifying gratifying conclusions of others
….So busy , that they missed the highlighted depict sent there way….
When would it end, your vicious of over spoken words you would
say…..No one asked you anyway…

Complicated Pleasures

Pleasure, is the outcome of something that brings a rather delightful enjoyment…..It only becomes complicated, as one throws in a twist that disturbs the flow in which it may contour….A mixture of rare confusion of order in which they must stay….It becomes more complicated, as you journey in a more serious way…Complicated pleasures, poured out to devour unfavorable complicated to mind….

Compromise

It took all I had to give just a little and not to take as once before…One
of such selfishly contour….I agreed to bend some, if you would come
and meet me half way with just a snitched this way…Defined as a beg
to sway one over this way with some incentive awaiting them at the
end……We shook hands, promising to do each parts, as we turned
around and walked away feeling somewhat a twisted way….When all
was said and put to it true test, it was a compromise we would lead

Crystallized Change Coming

As you journey through life, wandering what may be awaiting you, in this extravagant way…Nothing truly crystal clear as you would have hoped it to be….As you got through this and that, leaving you to make change to get the next….It is crystallized , that you are becoming more sufficient with the things that mattered ….One day in this, the next day in that…Change a coming, so fasten on and embrace your inner subjections as you bring a crystallized change in this light….

Don't Go There

I could deal with so many moods and ways of doing but, definitely
not right out bluntly overly spoken words just any kind of way….A lie
is a lie, with another to follow it in its deformed way…You ought be
who you were truly originated to be and not fake the funk on some
delusional trump …..Trying to handle as you are to be, don't go there,
for the peace may depart from thee…Another mood came over me, as
now I have been taken out of true self, quite indeed…No need to dress
it up to only undress what you told…Don't go there, for let it be told,
you caused a tremendous dare….Something overtaking, with such
empowerment that poured out of my inner fold….Come on now, don't
act like you had not been told, I spoke with directness when I spoke to
thee…

Don't Live in Regrets

Some many opportunities wished for and hoped for, but never sought the fight to grab hold to it…..I could turn the times back, I would embrace every opportunity that would elevate me to the next big success…If there was a intuition to follow through, don't under estimate the thought but better equip self to what is required in you, to do you…Live everyday, for if it was your last…So take hold to opportunities now, for they may not come back just for you….A lot of wish I could have and should oaf's, but no I did do's….Put yourself out there, into the unfamiliar zone….

Don't Walk Away

For there are still unfinished cares in the air…Don't walk away, for I never expressed my gratitude of your love you conveyed repetitiously to thee…For everything you have shown, never went un noticed to me…I need you, I need you, to be my shining light with the armor in the night….You were my hero, for I cherished every second with thee, for all we know it could be our last…So lets hit replay, the image of us in dire bare happiness like once before…Don't walk away, for I never want to say my good byes, so I say until we meet again my sweet…..

Don't You Dare

I could deal with so many moods and ways of doing but, definitely not right out spoken words that are in the form of a lie….Don't you there, for you may bring forth another displace me….I come in directness towards thee, leaving those afflictive issues where they may lay against thee…

Don't you go there, for something overtaking empowered the inner being to retaliate against thee…Come on real full with self and the rest fall where it may…

Elegance of One

As you sit there like you were on the finest jet magazine cover ready to pose, It took no artificial coloring of ones outer being, just your mere natural beauty glowed as if you only knew…It was spontaneous, like the perfect picture you could snap from Kodak make….You appeared stunning, as there was a view of astonishment…Not to say, you could never appear in this way, but there was nothing that equipped me for what I would say….Oh my, your extravagant glare caught me across the room as there I dared to stare…Elegance of one, was captivating to one….

Expressions

This is like poetry to me…It is passionate….It is like art where is you are the creator of all, you mold it into a captivation piece of art into the beholders eye…It is hypognathous of the mind from one soul of energy to another, like the static from your clothes…It is clingy to you then me and sensual in one….It is art and can be created the Burger King Way …Your way ….Expressions on one…

Father versus Daddy

A father Is a man, who has his named signed on the line, of who which he aided, in the creative self being...Does this really mean, he has it in him to be the man he was originated to be...Leaving me the resolution hat he would meet the past he set out to be...Another male that took part in the completion of that beautiful creation the other sought out to be....

A daddy is just that one, that contributed has seed to bring life but not to finish what was started to the light...

First Day at School

I was working overtime with the excitement of the anticipation of who or what the new teacher would be…Would they be uptight and not truly passionate of what I might ask of them, on this first day and the next after…..I just might be the one, that would ask a question every time there was some light brought to this observation…..I wandered, would this get on one's nerves or bring an impressive delight , that I was even the slightest concern in what it might open my mind with knowledge never absorbed before….My full intentions from the start was to, give it all I had, even if it might turn me inside and out with all my mite….

Forever Imprisoned

So often we find ourselves allowing our failures or just snare zones....We go on and on to question, what to be.....For all this torture was only meant to longer for one night and joy surly comes in the morning...There was no need to continually worry your inner concession, for it wouldn't change your already predestined steps arranged for your life....It is up to you, to take just one step out of that depicted grey that calls itself home....So what, you were just in the wrong place at the wrong time , only to stumble on mishaps to fins yourself all alone...Stand up for you, and tell everything and everyone that shined on you, that life moves on to the new the betterment for you....Perhaps, you have become quite comfortable in your imprisoned zone....unfortunately, this leaves one forever imprisoned in a lost caused zone...

Genuine Concern

There are truly one's that seek out your best interest at heart…There are one's that just want to know what you know there in….

Who would have a genuine concern, for what, and where I might go in the end….There are one's that take a walk as you walk into the next there in…They would never switch over to something new, but remains complex as if you already knew…Genuine, concern or simply attempting to know what I know….

Going on your feelings or on one's Faith

Your feelings go up and down so frequently, that you cant keep up with the suspense in which it will go...One minute you are feeling happy and then you are feeling down....W hat triggered this sudden abrupt change to come up rather observed....Setting out on the right now feelings, could lead one into a sudden drive into what appeared to be around...Stepping out to a another rim of feeling, such as one's faith of what cant be touched at this given moment in time....What will you do, Go on your feelings now or have some faith to things that are hoped for but not seen....

Hopeful Cause

We try o help all that we see and become dismayed of when we strike out….Hopeful cause as we sat out once again to reach to others as you would seek….Never giving up, never giving in, as you approach the cause once again…Hopeful cause, would make an everlasting impression that would linger within ones heart to thee….

I Missed You

Every second, every minute that passes me by, I became more reluctant to all your attributes that you offered to me as it appeared to be….Each second, be comes more profound, than the last, as I try to intersect the time divine…The point of it all, your absence left a forever lasting profound missing you aloud

I was Just Checking

Have not talked to you in a while….What have I missed from one's inner piece my dear…What new journey's have you, sought out since our last conversation I thought …What us the driven force behind your daily course of action….I was just checking, I was just checking, to see if you were fine….

If You Wandered Why

As I pondered a while, deciphering who it would be…You were chosen, to convey in such a gratifying way, with your heart-warmed designed within you to stay…If you were wandering why, it was your manner in you to put others first in a special way…You were chosen , for your charming wit you held within as you would convey to others that surround you each and everyday ….You stood out, more than the rest, because of your inner beauties that seemly couldn't rest…..As you entered a room full of emptiness, the positive energy that you posses generated over to others as they sit in rest….Your qualities that you bestowed inside, were what made your character so uplifting inside…..
If you wandered why, It was who you are with great uniqueness inside….

Inner Ambition

I longed for more than what I have…Never prolonging too long, on
the what or how's….I dreamed of fulfilling my fullest passion…It
was the vision that beat steadfast as it pattered the rushing urgency
of the inner energies corrupting the inner soul….May the power be
vested from the depths there in, as I vomited all of thy inner linings
of fulfillments through the inner ambitions within….It overflowed
like the dams river with a overflowing devour….

It Stops Right Here

You approached me with the friendless gestures with only to be sweet
to thee…For every word muttered from you, sounded like something
unheard…Needless to say quite impression in everyway….No tired
out begging lines trying to accomplish one thing something out of
the capacity of where we meet…Quite frank, I didn't give you the
assumption that I wanted more than a friendly talk in the rare…But
you, made it rather big and it stops right here instead….

Just Your Existence

You worked so hard to learn all you could hope to know...Only to be told you were not good enough...

What a derange formality, you would have thought...Needless to say, heartless and cold straight to the heart....Wow, is what you exclaimed, and what do you mean.....Just your existence, was what that appeared so openly in this ark....Crowds of people with ambitions that seemed quite anxious to rise above all they could meet...Just your existence, Just your existence, rather rare, rather extravagant to everyone that would stare....Your self esteem poured out the ugliness at a head... You wanted truly nothing but, just another day as we speak...No true aspirations you cared to meet, but seeking an easy place to beat....No one owed you nothing, as you expected exclaiming in such aurora... You seemed a little shock, when nothing absorbed from your rather dead ambitious that stare you at the door....With the formatted formula added in, nothing from nothing will surely give you a nothing ...Just your existence is left, what a quite smear impression you left in the air....

Kisses from the Unknown

I was mesmerizing, by all if the gestures passes to thee...You looked and pondered for a while the qualification of one to approach you...I hardly knew of you, just your kisses you would sway my way... Kisses from the unknown, are brought to you unknowingly to this zone...I was touched deeply, by your rather odd but sweet mere kisses you given me....Who was it, why was it....You sought thee... Kisses from the unknown.....

Let's Try Again

Your mere being, um left one in an ah…It is was a wonder, it didn't occur before now, the you and I ….We were friends until now… However, we entered this new chapter with the slowest precautions, worried that we were going to cross too many lines that we couldn't get the us back as we use to be….Lets try again, as the chemistry collaborates with the magic intercede as we spoon wrap each other ….You told me, you never felt this way before, for I knew you were jiving me, as you just knew the right words to say when they ought to be…Lets try again, for this may never come for you and me ever again…

Love Hard and Loving Easy

Your mere presence, was an extravagant glance into the loveliness one could ever see....I was taken back with your gestures, you conveyed to thee...Loving so easy, well one would say or maybe just loving hard from the first sight...I would care to follow...Your forever tenderness, made loving hard and easy so natural in this I must say....

Lusting Souls

You felt something tingling as if you medicated all over and seeking the removal of pain if told…Wandering why a love couldn't fit into that…You stayed delusional of all the fantasy that only one could think on….Wow, is the first initial thought as you tried to remove it from your head…You were taken back by your twinkle in your eye…You had seemly undressed my entirety as you stared for a moment at a time…I quickly asked what was birth sign to see where you would send in… Not much on folk tales, but truly it would tell where you fixing to head next in this depictive cell….Hearts of the dark and ran from the newness of light as others would be able to see in this rather rare status brought from opposite heart ..Lusting souls, where love had no centripetal home….

Mathematically Speaking

No efforts with little work, bring about no rewarding gratifying feeling to one in any way...Much effort with a tremendous great deal of works, go further around....Leaving one of fulfillment within and happiness there in....Mathematically speaking, zero plus zero, leaves a sum of a big ole nothing. While one plus one gives you more than you started with in a sum...

Mesmerize

I did all I could to stay in tact…As I saw you from across I looked, you took me back as you smiled with a full grin…Shaken, from the outer covering depict right in front of me…So refreshing, as I indulge your conversational of such delightful words…You were always, so nicely dressed with the nicest fragrance that would drive me wild…

My Dad's Love

He reached tall like a tree growing to the skies...He held us all together even when there was no promising words that would convince him to stay...He made ways for us all, even if he had to take one step back from self and await another to hold...He stepped in harms way, so that we each be safe in every which way...He simply spoke to us from what he would hold in with sincerity speaking we could hold...Even when, he was working hard to hold the foundation firm, he would take small breaks in between to tell each of us he loved us as a whole...My dad's love, was a shining light to hope for we could uphold....No other around, no other unsung with the tranquilities it bestrode in the threefold ...Your first impression was the ending impression I would pictured in my inner hold...

No Performance

The lights of the factional motions that take presence in front center stage….I yield, first to a father that sits high and low…Without one's permission, all else would fail….Through my everyday endeavors of the kindness deeds you would say…Never looking for not one thing in return…It was true, that one could sincerely give so much of oneself un conditionally…This was no performance, for it mattered not who would be my audience, for I gave from the depths from within and nothing could change that imparting spirit there within….

Nothing Else Left to Say

You have taken all the pureness of my inner sides, that I wish you hadn't done in this way…..You thought of yourself, as one of much eagle and cleverness that was untouchable in any way……It disturbed me of your arrogance of the lack of respect you carried out in your own way… You were such a pity sight , every time, I laid eyes on your intolerable ways….I disliked every ounce of your ways and attempted to have love for you in a different way…It took so much out of me, It wrecked me …..Astonishing, on how one person could do so much damage to the inevitable soul….Or more importantly, how one could allow one to do so, but as , epiphany stepped in with the reluctant to take back all that was mysterious stole from one's enemy untold…You have scared the inner soul, but I regained my true purpose of happiness to self in a threefold….It was the inner motivation there in that, made me know I was an unique creation sent from above...I cherished this , so there is nothing else left to say, let the truth be told……

Obsession

Things that surround your inner circle, that you seemly have clanged to without a clueless thought….You could not see nothing else around what was captivating thee…What an astounding image of regards to understanding life….You saw things in a one- sided eye glass , just unrealistic images of what you thought was right, to hold immersing close to you with no fear…It was in your head as you seemly shut one eye to sleep , as it steadfast beat you my dear.…..What is it, an obsession that is overtaking with a type of empowerment that gives you no sight…..It leaves one, feeling like there is a handicap that has crippled thee in their human might…..No thought of anything else, but this thing or that is overtaking you with its full power and might ….

Out of Anger

Spoken words we exchanged after withheld anguish inside…We spoke aloud of such faultless encounters we both had encountered in many ways…..Afterwards there were heart felt emotions that ran un tamed in a vindictive way…We both agreed, if only we had paused, then said our thoughts of expressions out of hate….There would have been a peace contemplated there in…..Spoken words of out of anger, can hit you like a sword with a sharp blade….Think first and act later with a peaceful spoken word…

Out of Courtesy

I was surrounded by your mere presence constantly, but never a lot
to say to you in conversation on any day......Surly I would say, a brief
greet of hello to you and I am doing fine...It was something about you
that just didn't rub me the right way...You could have spoken a few
words and that was enough for me to hear in any way....I was just
being kind to you, because they was the way I was taught....Never no
one, I would hang out with in a frivolous way ..Out of courtesy, is all I
can say......

Perfect Harmony

When things mingled together without an extra touch…When you know the words I was getting ready to say before I finish… When you become brand new within self and new attitude in touch … Perfect Harmony, as we reunite as one in this nation…As we walk into prosperity of new wealth's soon to come….

Please Forgive Me

For all the wrongs that I have committed and through ultimately your way…..Never keeping an precise count of all that was commenced all to you which was done…..Lord how mercy, were the words spoken from the sincerity from the deepest part of my inner heart….I thought of no one else's feelings, when I committed, that overpowering act… Unknowing, the impact that it would have on you, in only one single act….It was not that I didn't have a heart, of what damage it would have created to you in a distort way… As each moment passed and the hours propagated into days, I knew that I had to make forgiveness plea in a special way…I am sorry, so please forgive me if you find a place to do so in this I earnestly say….I have done you wrong in a quite distort way….For I have realized the previous wrong doings from my wickedness way, so convey my deepest regret of the harm I may have brought your way….

Profound Statement

With much emphasis of what thought you dared to express with high
priority to all…It stood out like a soar thumb where all others could
take a glance…Its words so powerful, it was full of improvement
for the inner soul….Afterwards, leaving one fully impacted with a
forever lasting impression there within the depths with such a great
profound….

Racial Contradictive

Mixture of blends from all over with the combos of black, white, Hispanic , Korean , Japanese , or even Arabic with an even disbar…. Racial contradictive, left millions speechless from the start…Some not willing to be open minded about another side of the multi love culture to blend contradictive with glee…When love pours out, it knew not the color that was opposed completive on thee…It embraced all that would grab hold to thee…All that truly mattered, was that the respect be true to thee…For all others could stop and stare, as the Racial Contradictive leaves a marked impressive thought….

Rain Down on Me

As the wetness, poured from the inner bare, you were astonished by the tranquilities liquids that was unpredicted in the forecast...Rain down on me, rain down on me, as the excitement creates an explosive interceding the inner me....Occupied with the astonishment of the reexamining of this way and within as the rain surpasses even more...Rain down on me, rain down on me, as the forecast meets the expected destined for the inner me....

Reaction to your Actions

For every course of reaction, surly there is a setback affirmation that intertwine with your given action...

Enter with immersing precautions as you played a little too long with that god forbidden zone...Be careful what you ask for truly your wish may be done and be even more yielding to whom you laugh at, for this could in return point back to you....Reaction to your action, leaving one rather stung in the off set that you just begun... For every action, it deserves a reaction...

Rebellious Child

As I venture out to new adventures in life, in which I rebelliously
relinquished from inside....I knew the general format of the what ifs to
be exact...Rather than being in the right, I would rather do wrong......
As many times, I was told no, I would find some way to say yes to my
inner soul.....So caught up in what I chose to hold, and could careless
of what I know I had been told....I set out in many formalities, as
they would unfold, to drive full force in what awaited to unfold...
Many lessons, came as I frivolously created messes all over in such a
threefold.... Rebellious Child, Rebellious Child, full of a broken spirit to
what is best for me....

Reposition Oneself

A thoughtful word, once uplifted one's zest in every way…Your associated surroundings created a character in one…Be careful who you allow to be in your inner circle, as you sought your purpose for self all alone.…..As failures, would come one by one, but only for you to knock them out all in one…As your journey on to what await you next….The reposition of self will somber one's heart, as you traveled along this somber less road…..Reposition oneself, to another reconstructive work zone……

Resolutions

As each of you smother on the mere thought of what it I you would like to start your new beginning with….Look at the mere idea of what suits you and not others…Making your resolution personal to you, set only expectations that contour the real you….In doing so, you will find, the reality of it all, depends on one's mindset in a special way…..

Revengeful Heart

In a lifetime of journey's traveled, there were plenty of enemies accumulated and a plenty of friends made…So many paths crossed, of the un liking hearts combined trivia from one…As I tried to be kind, the brutality rested in the state of a revengeful heart there in…The heart of converted wicked soul, lives for moments at a given time…. Through the revengefulness, nothing would be sought, but troubles in the valleys from this moment there in….

Romantic Dinner

The candles are prearranged for two, as you anticipate the mood...
Lovers and friends if it was let known....The music is collaborated
in a imagined scene of Romance set alone...As silence broke across
the room, as the mood was beginning to manifest love of its own....
As we intertwine each others exchanged sensual thoughts, the love
made its own....Who knew where this would lead us from which this
movement originated its formality from.... At the moment, we cared
less of the formality that would manifest in itself......

Silent Voice

As moments had passed, leaving the sense of urge at its begging call, with no dire regrets...The unspoken words, went unannounced, as the actions were quite appealing...The body language is what was watched from ashore...It replaced the vicious words from raining souls...It was the silent voice, that stood out in a rather prudent content than before... The silence, brought about the miraculous reactions from the inner soul, leaving one rather puzzled with great amour...

So many Times

You have given suggestive wisdom, that remained hidden forever more…Needless to say you repetitiously speak life into what was already presumed dead, so you thought…So many times, there was silence that grew across one's lips…Never knowing what you would find out, from the outer source that spoken a word too…Leaving one rather confused with a great heap of a sigh…Questioning one's self ability to tell the difference of what, where, and how so many times, you dared to throw a silent ear to what was in dire need …So many times , it ran rarely deep there in, wandering when this too would vanish away, after so many times in a quite different way…

Soul Search

Taken a break for a bit of a while, with others seemly moving through life with determined destinations with strengths of ambitions that are just waiting to unfold….With precautious proceeding to my revived you….Living in the uncertain of now, as I rectify what was just resting inside….refusing to allow talents that have been gifted to me from way above from the heavens which were blue…Learning there is a time and place in which things would come to play….As I continued on my soul search, it became crystallized on what I wanted on this journey relinquished in a whole….

Speaking From the Heart

As I began to speak what it be from the inner thee…I loosely disclose my inner tuition of thee….I found it useless to silence one's lips spoken from thee…No time for the false perception conveyed outwards to thee….In doing this, it would take away the trueness in me…Forgive me, for loosely giving away the word that were conveyed to me in every which way…I speak from the inter session of love through the deeper depths there in one's soul….

Stepping Out In the Unknown

As the human flesh set in, it makes us completive in a comfort zone in such an amour...A comfort zone, that has made itself right at home... Never knowing, where this day may take one in such a adventurous place...

Fear, remained the top factor as I journeyed along with all the challenges that would come my way...When stepping out into unknown zones, the depictive perception of limitations, was immediately made to move from my way...Living with the expectations, for more than previous journeyed in the lifetime lived just moments before....For a change in one's inner soul, left the excitement of the unknown anticipation unknown....Opportunities, are here now and may never present them selves in this formality ever again.... Stepping out in the unknown zones, the zone of higher expectations with strong driven ambitions reserved for thee...

Stop Judging Ourselves

We are our worse critics, in attempting to line our subdue lives on a judging poll….Giving ourselves the third degree….We have yet failed to realize, that we all have mistakenly failed along the way…Giving no credits to the true attributes that dwell in the inner side….No allowance, to the inner growth that blossomed all over inside…As I sat back and watches the real me pour out all its sincerity's from a deeper distinctive outward side…Stop judging ourselves, quite contrary, leaving an emptiness inside.….

Stuck on Stupid

What is it , What is it that you didn't get as I first spoke to thee....
You act as if you a little slow...What is it, Stuck on Stupid or what
....Some people just cant move along to what awaits, because they
are still in the past that has already taken its place...As if you could
change the past of the what was...Rather than to make way to change
to the now rather than the later...However, if not, I guess that leaves
you stuck on stupid ....You have a free chose with all sorts of options
that would effect the new you when it is all said and done....

The Detour

Once we preset our own destinations, that sometimes follows a detour
of some sort to proceed....We, had already hyped our inner source of
what we believed so hard in and could obvious see no other routes
in doing so in no depicted way...We fell a deaf ear to what signs,
that were presented to us in its own distinctive way ....As it stood
forefront in front of our way, we walked around it and kept on going
in our own set out ways......These, symbolic signs were presented
to us from god, to help avoid tragedy heading our way......We were
warned numerous of times, so that we would not have to destroy the
inner ambitions that we set out adjourn...Trying to save us from self
of things that were truly unseen, that were coming straight for us in
its own way...The Detour, is to allow another way to your destination
without having to contour the inevitable events that were just waiting
to shake us with discouragement to deviate from what was good in a
miraculous way ....

The Dire Passion

The burning feeling of realizing you were wanting more…..It would
not let me sleep as it pitter patter against me as I would sleep…It came
across my mind as I carried out the inner confession within my soul…..
It behooves my inner intellectual as I mold it into what I hold deep
there in….The dire passion, runs deeper as the times moves on….When
I start to do what I believed to be next, it kept returning its truthful
passion indeed

Trail and Error

Never traveled through so unseen tunnels of life…Not knowing what awaits me at the end…The chance in which I was willing to take with many upper hands….Trial and error, was the best given solution to this unusual circumstances…. I attempted this and then that, unknowing what to truly expect…If I first don't succeed, try, try again indeed… Trial and error….There is surly, to be better next time….

Tranquilities

I sat out on a voyage of a mission of a misplaced certain something or someone….It never came through in my set out mission of you….I wandered for a prolonged moment, where could it be and carried out another search for you….I was quite astonished of your absence and grew reluctant of you….Where could you be, I wandered with great weary of where you might be….I continued on the mission of your where you might be located in a few journeys of the depict place of a many ….It appeared that you were hiding from one and there were others that I came across in my search for that certain search of you….I took hold of the substitute, that came forefront view….It was the original mission, but I guess I would settle for it and go on to what was right there all along …..

Triumphs

So many trials, so many errors in thy ways…We feared the one thing most knew of, our challenges that faced us face to face in everyway… We wish to run and even hide, but never coming to realization, that we can with stand the test to become a complete success….No one knows where the road or journey will go, but you will never know its full reward, if you never run this road…Triumphs in one, are far too many to let it be wasted to another untold….

Undefined Line

The curiosity kills the cat as you anticipate the unexpected all along...No true dry cut explanation, but hints sent your way...You make inquiry' s of all sort to figure things out....You were intense on knowing things, but surprises are truly undefined...What was the point in this matter , one would say...Others would just go with the flow in any which way....Could be this or that in these unspoken words undefined this way...Unsolved mysteries, waiting to be solved by all of our private investigators in this deranged funky fide way...

Under The Influence

You fell into a deep sleep which left you unconscious for a prolonged moments…You became quite numb all over, as things began to spun all around you….No response from one, as others took advantage of your complete being …As you tried to bring yourself to, you were rather clueless of what to do, so you did nothing ..Under influence, of some other over taking spirit that would capture you in a rather captivating freeze of what you thought…..What had happened to you, what an astonishing thought…..As one awaited for the answer, time was surly slipping away, now there got to be some other way….Under the influence , in a over powering way…

Unraveled Spirit

As I encountered millions as we speak ...Some clashing my inner
soul, some lifting me to be more than the last and there is others that
would like steal what I have in me....No matter, what seemed to be the
cause, the unraveled spirit manifested in great delight...People, often
wandered, what was my secret of relinquishing the inner true me...
It was quite simple, I chose to toss all that was out my control and
steer my energy in the spirit to seek out to touch others despite...Some
would embrace this with openness and others would surly become
deaf ear to this sight

We Will See

So many ideas spoken amongst us all, so many promises given but only a few to be followed....All with great intentions, but quite rare to be brought to light….The theory of jumping too far ahead, came to mind when the focus to follow through became rather dead…Will see, what was to follow or what fell off one's unsung lips in the brightness of light, for we will see

What Came Over Me

I been waiting on you all day, mentally ravishing thoughts of us spoon hugged in thee…Wanting to try everything kinky there was to meet…. You digging it, for just wanting to explore your every compulsive snafu that I was willing and able to mold…What came over me, what came over me, I imagined you most indecisive bare exploding like the volcanoes air …You appeared weary, for what I would dare…Turning you inside and out without any hesitation in this dilation…. I was ready to take hold newest endeavor, grabbing an inch and then another, leaving you to be….No not really just bull jiving your mental gravity in thee…What came over me, I tell you feeling my inner sexual tee… Yearning that closeness all around me…..Needing you, totally, so don't you dare hold any out from me….

What Did You Say

So many contradictive words came swinging my way….No true
definitions, could be found…They rolled under the bare knits of my
skin that truly brought a disruption all around….I could of said so
many things, but I chose to give silence instead….What did this truly
say, it gave me a moment to regain a thought of one or two…What did
you say, a lot of empties in an extra ordinary way ….Nothing, was
needed to be said, just silence….

What is your Given Purpose

We all at some point or another have doubted your purpose on earth......We seemly torture ourselves with un answered questions we have prearranged, to only get omit to the next...we set out on numerous endeavors, wishing and hoping to find that something or someone to fulfill that void...What is your given purpose, what is your given purpose, so many thoughts into this one, we asked our mothers, fathers, sisters, and even those brothers...No one really had clear cut reasoning, on what was to be done or even to do.....What is your given purpose, it is to full fill each assignment to its fullest until the next makes itself to be known....Surly, you would not allow your mind to set at peace with this, so don't just dwell on such, but rather, go on the assumption that the journey is full of exciting unknown zones never traveled entered into before.....

What Keeps Me Going

I start my daily with a prayer of hope and peace for the inner too much more…What keeps me going, I awake to other persons that depend heavenly on thee…They call me mommy and wait for the thoughtful word for the day…I would relate these words in such a meaningful way, be leader and not a follower to others that watch you when you call yourself being discreet….When attempting, one assignment and the outcome may not be what I thought it ought to be…I began again, to the next task with more driven power than before…What keeps me going, I feel the energy form me to you as I hand down to you the prayer of hope that never cease with much derivation to thee….

What Makes You a Delight

It is your incredible compassion you give from your heart...Your tenderness you share with others leaving a mark...Your kind words that you convey expressively in a magnificent way...What makes you a delight, your rarity so hard to find ....So I desire its pleasurable delight.....

What you do to me

I can feel every rib moving as you move with the body's music…I feel you caressing every inch of my bare, as you slither your mere tender lips along my linings…It brings a delight of such indulgent all over… Sexual as it may feel, it leaves me anticipating the next for more…As you come to a conclusion, you're bare against mine…Ravish me, I am saying give me more, give me more…At your request, I am giving you a standing ovation, well done, well done my sweet….

When it was all said and Done

After our constant disagreements, night after night < I cried endlessly with bloody eyes…Fighting, to just keep my sanity with an open eye…

When it was all said and done, we both knew what had to be done, with no love remaining, it was clear that we needed to depart…I often wandered , could anyone here my humble cry, oh how I wanted to leave him indeed, but just didn't know how to say….One thing was clear, I loved him hard & over easy, until I placed myself into this pity dungeon where it was put aside…..When it was all said and done, I realized that I had not indeed weighed the pros and cons….For all the hatred and bitterness, needed a new place to call its rightful home…. When it was all said and done, my life was indeed really mine and it was worth the chance I would take to regain newness of mine…

When Will It Be

You say you want change , but you stand in its way….Then you sit there and ask when will it be….You repetitiously repeat, I want change, I want change to come for me….Needless to say, you make no effort in allowing it to be so…..You want things to come as quick as they can, but no true commitment to your change when it unfolds…..Say what you mean and then allow it to uphold….When will it be, this cant be happening to me….For one step leads to another step, and then the change manifests itself in a whole….This is when it will be….

When you Lose A Love One

The time had suddenly approached abruptly, as my dear loved one,
was sweep away, before I had a chance to say goodbye in a magnificent
way…So much I wanted to convey to you, of your love that glowed in
a special way….However, through you sent an angel to me, whispering
in this to say, no need to fret, for I knew just how you felt about me, but
the inner know that I am free with the peace there in the depths of my
consoled soul in a better way….

Words

Words, consists of various letters that define what is needed to express a thought of some kind …They know no particular order, in which they should convey, so guide them in their proper way….Unknowingly, they may come across rather strong, leaving one feeling all alone…It may even come across as uplifting, in a strange depicted way….They may come high pitched, low pitched, or even pitched as each letter is arranged in their own defined way….They travel through the mid open skies, as they fly swooping by…The words in which you speak, determines the intellectual of one in its own defined way….Words here now, and in the near future, so lets make it our very special own….

Wrongly Accused

There were plenty of persons that it could have been, but seemly everyone, had pretty much come to there own conclusion, that it was me without a second thought….There was no true investigation that would lead one to believe that it could have been me….A mystery of why was there nothing that would stick out and persuade them in another way…..Could there have been some little piece missing from the already facts that were obviously not sorted through to come up with some truths…….There were several years that had passed, that I would wear this, accused wrongly that is…

You Knew Nothing

So quick to always speak what you thought we all should hear…. Never stopping a moment, to sort through the ending conclusion there in….You were one of such argument point of views that shared many opinions from plenty that knew…You were never wrong, in anything, for everything you spoke was believed to be true, so you thought, you knew…..When all was said, you were so far from right and you knew nothing not really …You were completely in denial of what lied there strong ahead, but let it be known, you knew nothing and attempted to make it something….

You were my First

It was awaited for what seemed a lifetime full of a test....I eyed you staring me as I glanced at you in the wrong....Needless to say, you would had never came clean on what it was that you saw in me...So, I made the gumption, of approaching you with such a delusive way, you never knew what just happened...Taken you completely off guard, and you were taken by the breathe of fresh air that just hit your mentality bare...You were indeed my first that I dared to step out like never before.....

Your Journey

As you travel through distort that the world has laid upon us, there in the mist of it, remains a crystallized depict, heading one's way.... Take hold to it and absorb all its opportunities for uplifts of even more success in every way...